A Second Look Around

Marie Moser

BookLeaf
Publishing

India | USA | UK

A Second Look Around © 2023 Marie Moser

All rights reserved.

No part of this publication may be reproduced, stored in a retrieval system, or transmitted, in any form or by any means, electronic, mechanical, photocopying, recording or otherwise, without the prior written permission of the presenters.

Marie Moser asserts the moral right to be identified as author of this work.

Presentation by *BookLeaf Publishing*

Web: www.bookleafpub.com

E-mail: info@bookleafpub.com

ISBN: 9789358736694

First edition 2023

*This is for all of those who stayed and fought
the war. And for one who was just visiting for a
time but will never be forgotten.*

Redemption

Will you be my scapegoat?
Will you take the blame?
Will you undertake to house
My bitterness and pain?
Will you hold my hand, dear?
Will you understand?
Will you accept that nothing here
is working out as planned?
Will you let me rest, love?
Will you let me sleep?
Will you hold against me
All the lies I tried to keep?
Will you let me wander?
Will you pin me down?
Will you be the rock or
Can you help me not to drown?
Will you walk beside me?
Will you let me stall?
Will you hold me accountable
For every time I fall?
Will you let me cry now?
Will you call my name?
Will you help me recognize
There's healing from the shame?

Villanelle #1

I know that you are not at home.
Shrieking, stalking, preying at your door.
And now I'll cry and die alone.
This emptiness shall chill my bones.
Upon rage, resentment I will pour.
I know that you are not at home.
To murder now my thoughts have flown.
Grisly, gruesome vestment that I wore.
And now I'll cry and die alone.
Tis madness now has set this tone.
Endless plots have overfilled my stores.
I know that you are not at home.
False tenderness now fixed in stone.
Cast about for tainted love no more.
And now I'll cry and die alone.
Obscured, my soul remains unknown.
No hesitance, darkness shall explore.
I know that you are not at home.
And now I'll cry and die alone.

Welcome To My Life

Horrendous nighttime.
Perform the mad drunk knife dance.
And the cigarette.

Panic midday fear.
Chair empty, rhythm dulls pain.
Strangers see no lie.

Warming evening Beckoning,
hazy phone sings.
And holding the glass.

Early day breaks free.
Lonely bed cries for double.
Betrayed by the truth.

Screaming darkness cries alone.
Fuzzy vague cannot atone.

Aging Gracefully

Living in denial does not the clock stop.
Fading, noiseless, relentless each day.
Using makeup and hairstyles and friends as a
prop.
Any excuse I can find to delay.
The crazy cat lady is such a cliché.
One day you'll search but I'll not be found.
I don't want to leave but I know I can't stay.
Time falls away till I'm cold in the ground.

Nervous Abecedarian

Aqua is for accepting all the things I cannot
change.
Black resembles hatred, for familiar now feels
strange.
Crimson stands for fear that things will never be
the same.
Denim is for lonely: when I cried out no one
came.
Emerald means relaxed in the faith that things
night heal.
Fuscia stands for sexy, which is how I used to
feel.
Grey is for disgust that I still love you when you
bite.
Harvest feels so bitter, like I've given up the
fight.
Ivory is trusting, which I was when this thing
started.
Jade stands for the pride I lost the moment that
we parted.
Khaki means revulsion at the turn my life has
taken.
Lime is for excitement that some have not
forsaken.

Mauve feels like the shame when I recall the
things I said.
Navy stands for exhausted – I just want to go to
bed.
Orange resembles funny. I have to laugh so I
don't cry.
Pink stands for the strength to hold my own and
not comply.
Quartz feels confused at this capacity for pain.
Ruby means furious that I'm held down by these
chains.
Silver stands for confidence that I may make it
through.
Taupe is for insulted for some think that that's
untrue.
Ultramarine feels so heavy, like this weight will
pull me down.
Violet means surprise since there's a chance I
might not drown.
White fades to hopeless. Could this really be the
end?
Xanadu is anxious that I don't deserve my
friends.
Yellow stands for happy since I know that I will
make it.
Zucchini resembles guilt because I know I'll
have to fake

Exclamation of Life

If I could choose my punctuation, what would I
be?
Perhaps a comma, joining two ideas together is a
cohesive fashion.
Maybe a colon, presenting the impetus for a
succinct explanation.
I might choose a period, indicating there is no
further cause for argument.
Finality.
How about an apostrophe, with the ability to
both indicate possession and ownership and omit
unnecessary detritus?
Most likely I would be an interrobang.
The overarching concept of life consisting of a
tragic comedy of
holy shit and what the hell is going on?

Letter To a Friend

The years I sacrificed for you.
I never will regret.
The moments that we shared alone.
I never will forget.
You lit a spark inside my heart.
I never dreamed existed.
We thought we'd make it through as two,
My loyalty enlisted.
You couldn't stand the honesty
My convictions would incur.
Instead you chose to run away
My sedition, you'd infer .
And now we stand alone and scared
Adrift amongst the flames.
You knew that I could not endure
The judgment without name.
I'll live and breathe my freest breath
Without the fear of silence
You alone can bring this peace
Without the threat of violence.

Your Move

The game is not fixed in your favour.
You have become blinded by your own hübris
and are incapable of detecting the strategies of
those who have risen above.
This self imposed blindness;
This...willful ignorance...will be your ultimate
reward.
How dare you diminish the light and spirit of
those so long unwilling to speak?
How dare you assume your role...
your
Position of control?
You fancy yourself a knight, a king
All powerful.
All encompassing.
For far too long this game has lingered.
Pawns dancing, deflecting, diminished at your
Utter gall and willingness to seize control
At any cost.
But, my dear friend, you underestimated your
foe.
For the desperate, limited, downtrodden pawns
have arisen.
Queens.
Stronger than any.

Than every.
This will not end in your favour.
But it will end.
You will at last realize defeat.
Your bitter medicine shall poison only your soul.
Powerless, you will concede.
There is no delight at your demise.
Only resignation.
This game cannot accompany a draw.
This pawn, now queen, shall survive your ill
intent.
Cower, fear and hide.
For you have achieved your zugzwang.

True Loss

Come on out it's time to play
Life's confusion gets in the way
I know the drink entices still
But we still love you if you will
accept the things that cannot change
we know we can still rearrange
The fate we choose is still alive
For the sake of our souls we still will thrive
The end is not yet in our sight
for we all know we've seen the light
Our petty fears we push aside
The rejection we will take in stride
The love we fear has all been lost
but still we count them in our cost
Our strength Our will we shall endure
but for our death there is no cure
Yet strive we will within our hearts
because we know if we should part
Our souls once linked will fall and die
if we do not accept that pride
will bring us to a merciless end
and kill the ones that we call friend
Our hearts connect make no mistake
So with our lives a chance we'll take
to tie us to our vast reward

and distance us from all discord
So let's hold hands and know we're right
and follow love into the light

My Babies

Just one look is all it took
for you to steal my heart.
And even though I sleep alone
I know we'll never part.
Your voice, your heart, your boundless love
sustained me through the pain.
And even though we are apart,
I'd do it all again.
Acceptance and affection
were your number one concern.
And to your sweet and loving arms
I always would return.
I knew that I count count on you
in every single way.
You loved and were loved in return
for each and every day.
You brought the light into my life,
you helped me find my song.
The musketeers, we conquered all.
We three could do no wrong.
Our friends we made along the way
became our family.
We added each like precious pearls,
fulfilling destiny.
I hear your voices in my dreams.

And feel your precious kisses.
Just know far up in heaven
that it's you that Mommy misses.
We'll meet again, my angels now,
But always in my soul.
And we know as far as I'm concerned
we achieved our greatest goal.
Our endless love and tenderness
was all we ever gave.
I never realized I
would be the one that you would save.
So till we meet again, my babies,
rest and no more pain.
I'll send my love and know
that I will see you both again.

The Nemesis

Do I drink the drink
Or does it drink me?
Tethered together
For eternity.
This dance is a game
No one can lead.
Just a brief respite
Is all I need.
I know its charms.
Does it lead or follow?
I feel its arms
With every swallow.
I've made my choice.
This is my end.
My ice filled cup
Is my lasting friend.
This love will last
With every sip.
For this sweet freedom
Is not a slip.
But a choice I've made
Just to survive.
This brief respite
Will help me live.
If I should go

Before my time.
Please rest assured,
The choice was mine.
Don't weep and moan
At my last rest.
For this old world
Gave me a test.
I passed and failed
At my expense.
They'll be no chance
For recompense.
But choose I did.
Now my reward.
This bittersweet
Is my sharp sword.
Do not dismay.
I loved you still.
Until the day
I've had my fill.
This love won't die.
Although it should.
These choices made
Do me no good.
But choose I shall.
This life's a choice.
My drug filled cup
Gives me no voice.
Perhaps I win.
Perhaps I'll die.

At least I'll know
The reason why.
I gave my all
For one last taste.
My life not led
To end in waste.
So don't you cry
When I depart.
You know that you
Possess my heart.
It's faster now.
So don't debate.
My destiny
Is sealed in fate.

Getting Played

When do we lose control?
Crafted, designed to sing, to exalt, to transcend.
As whole we are silent.
Nothing but potential.
Nothing but possibility.
Alone we cannot express our limitless ability to
bring forth
Life
Love
Death
Hope
Pain
Helpless without a plectrum – an impetus – a
thrust.
Without our quiddity, their purpose is fruitless.
Is ultimate power in the hands of the maestro
or the tool upon which he exerts his command?
Symbionts, we.
Existing only to elevate our latent talent,
Death in solitude.

Villanelle #2

Even blinded eyes will see
Distant illusions have vexed my mind.
Things are what they seem to be.
Spectres hazy now break free.
Fallacious images now align.
Even blinded eyes will see.
No delusion is my plea.
Pareidolia I am in inclined.
Things are what they seem to be.
Sanity from me shall flee.
Visions seek to solve but cannot find.
Even blinded eyes will see.
Scattered remnants now agree,
But only serve memories that bind.
Things are what they seem to be.
Flawed deceptions end with thee.
Tis mirage, these images entwined.
Even blinded eyes will see
Things are what they seem to be.

Treasure Hunter

Baseball glove to catch a pitch.
Floor length jacket made of fitch.
Ancient albums stuffed with pictures.
Pieces of electrical fixtures.
Hand carved soldiers made of wood.
A comic about Robin Hood.
A menu from a restaurant diner.
Some cushions from a bent recliner.
A necklace with now rusted metal.
A bicycle with just one pedal.
Pictures of animals someone drew.
Tales of heroic derring do.
Disorganized collections, unsystematic.
Will always be found in a dusty old attic.

Altered Reality

Our taxpayer dollars will make you quite rich.
Living in luxury can be such a bitch.
We suffer and scrimp to put food on the table.
While you drain our accounts as much as you're able.
You fools, you accuse as we stand for our rights.
While our capacity to speak truth is dead in your sights.
The powers you abuse are designed to control.
Our coffers run bare while your cupboards are full.
When we stand up and fight you go on the attack.
You're truly offended we dare to fight back.
Our children go hungry, you provide us no aid.
If we cause too much trouble you offer us MAiD.
You jet off on junkets on Canadian's dime.
And laugh at our charter rights you people designed.
Get jabbed or stay home are the options you give.
And encourage them all who deride how we live.

Religion and speech have been pushed
underground.
You fine us and jail us for making a sound.
Our pride in this country has taken a hit.
But freedom and a fire in our hearts have been
lit.
We'll shake off the shame and take back this
great nation.
You will fail at your goal of victimization.
So cower in fear, Justin, we're coming for you.
Our restitution is long overdue.
The small fringe minority has become the loud
voice.
And soon you will realize you don't have a
choice.
We'll march, honk and pray our way to
independence.
And you'll be forced to choose between death
and repentance.

Entitled Companions

Cats walk with aplomb
in the assurance that
they are the most important creatures on earth.
They're not wrong.

Call

Don't bother to love me,
I'm already gone.
We've already penned
all the words to this song.
We scratch and we bite
every time that we leap.
Let's give it a rest
so we both get some sleep.
There's more to the world
than the pain we inflict.
We lessen our worth
with the lies we depict.
I need to be free
to find out who I am.
You deserve better
than just half a man.
I'll spare you my journey.
I must walk alone.
The ones that I find here
will give me a home.
If fail or if folly
should find me a friend,
You won't be the one
upon which I depend.
I'll crack and I'll break

and I'll crawl to the light.
I'll come out the victor
or die in this fight.
Don't bother to love me.
I know you'll be fine.
The survival I'm worried
about now is mine.

Answer

I already love you.
You don't have to go.
We don't have to validate
this tale of woe.
The wounds we inflicted
will heal, given time.
Let's just know what matters:
I'm yours and you're mine.
We lash out in anger,
but our wounds will heal.
This blame we inflict
has a sordid appeal.
You want to be free
and I'm holding you back.
But soon you'll discover
it's love that you lack.
You think that your friends
will provide a safe space.
I'll wait till you realize
that I'm your best place.
You left me to find
all the things you could do.
I accept that your focus
was not me but you.
But I'm all alone now

and scared, don't you see?
The one that you left here
behind is just me.
So go on and play.
Find your wings, learn to fly.
This is more powerful
than just you and I.

One For The Road

"Try the wine" he advises.
I came in for a 6 pack of cheap beer.
Taco's and baseball and sweatpants wait at
home.
"White or red?" he doggedly insists.
"Dry or sweet? Bold or crisp? Bubbly or still"?
This jagoff fancies himself a sommelier.
Beer. I want beer.
Ballgame and greasy food and stocking feet.
Maybe he owns stock in a vineyard.
See, swirl, smell, sip,
slurp, savor, spit.
I don't care about complexity or finesse, but I do
need to pick up some hot sauce on the way
home.
Paper or plastic? Does it matter?
"Have a grape day!
Please come again"!
Not likely, my friend.

Purple Dreams of Abandon

I do not mean to be overly finical.
But when I hired a harpist,
I assumed that I would not have to
move a piano.

www.ingramcontent.com/pod-product-compliance
Lightning Source LLC
LaVergne TN
LVHW010845200726

843508LV00012B/2767